To:

From:

The Pocket Pooh

*Wit and Whimsy from the
World of Winnie-the-Pooh*

Text by A. A. Milne
Illustrations by Ernest H. Shepard

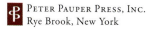

Peter Pauper Press, Inc.
Rye Brook, New York

PETER PAUPER PRESS
Fine Books and Gifts Since 1928

Our Company

In 1928, at the age of twenty-two, Peter Beilenson began printing books on a small press in the basement of his parents' home in Larchmont, New York. Peter—and later, his wife, Edna—sought to create fine books that sold at "prices even a pauper could afford."

Today, still family owned and operated, Peter Pauper Press continues to honor our founders' legacy—and our customers' expectations—of beauty, quality, and value.

Designed by La Shae V. Ortiz

Copyright © 2025
Peter Pauper Press, Inc.
3 International Drive
Rye Brook, NY 10573 USA

All rights reserved
ISBN 978-1-4413-4650-6
Printed in China
7 6 5 4 3 2 1

Visit us at www.peterpauper.com

The Pocket Pooh

Wit and Whimsy from the World of Winnie-the-Pooh

INTRODUCTION

"Once upon a time, a very long time ago now, about last Friday, Winnie-the-Pooh lived in a forest all by himself under the name of Sanders . . ."

This little book, filled with selections from *Winnie-the-Pooh* and *The House at Pooh Corner*, invites you into the Hundred Acre Wood and the charming

company of Pooh, Piglet, Eeyore, Rabbit (and Rabbit's numerous friends and relations), Owl, Kanga, Roo, Tigger, and Christopher Robin. Bask in the gentle humor, keen insights, and woodland wisdom within. A miniature keepsake, it fits perfectly in pocket, purse, or desk, offering comfort, joy, and wonder whenever needed.

"What about a story?" said Christopher Robin.
"*What* about a story?" I said.
"Could you very sweetly tell Winnie-the-Pooh one?"
"I suppose I could," I said. "What sort of stories does he like?"
"About himself. Because he's *that* sort of Bear."

Christopher Robin was sitting outside his door, putting on his Big Boots. As soon as he saw the Big Boots, Pooh knew that an Adventure was going to happen, and he brushed the honey off his nose with the back of his paw, and spruced himself up as well as he could, so as to look Ready for Anything.

*It's a very funny thought that,
    if Bears were Bees,
They'd build their nests at the
    bottom of trees.
And that being so
    (if the Bees were Bears),
We shouldn't have to climb up
    all these stairs.*

"What do I look like?"
"You look like a Bear holding on to a balloon," you said.
"Not," said Pooh anxiously—"not like a small black cloud in a blue sky?"
"Not very much."
"Ah, well, perhaps from up here it looks different. And, as I say, you never can tell with bees."

Bear began to sigh, and then found he couldn't because he was so tightly stuck; and a tear rolled down his eye, as he said: "Then would you read a Sustaining Book, such as would help and comfort a Wedged Bear in Great Tightness?"

"*What!*" said Piglet, with a jump. And then, to show that he hadn't been frightened, he jumped up and down once or twice more in an exercising sort of way.

PIKNICKS

KANGAS HOUSE

SANDY PIT WHERE ROO PLAYS

RABBITS HOUSE

POOH BEARS HOUSE

SIX PINE TREES

POOH TRAP FOR HEFFALUMPS

PIGLETS HOUSE

The Sun was still in bed,
but there was a lightness
in the sky over
the Hundred Acre Wood
which seemed to show
that it was waking up
and would soon be
kicking off the clothes.

"Because Poetry and Hums aren't things which you get, they're things which get *you*. And all you can do is to go where they can find you."

He sat down and thought, in the most thoughtful way he could think.

"Lucky we know the Forest so well, or we might get lost," said Rabbit half an hour later, and he gave the careless laugh which you give when you know the Forest so well that you can't get lost.

Piglet sidled up to Pooh from behind. "Pooh!" he whispered.

"Yes, Piglet?"

"Nothing," said Piglet, taking Pooh's paw. "I just wanted to be sure of you."

"And how are you?"
said Winnie-the-Pooh.
Eeyore shook his head from
side to side.
"Not very how," he said.
"I don't seem to have felt at
all how for a long time."

"Well," said Owl, "the customary procedure in such cases is as follows." "What does Crustimoney Proseedcake mean?" said Pooh. "For I am a Bear of Very Little Brain, and long words bother me."

"It means the Thing to Do."
"As long as it means that, I don't mind," said Pooh humbly.

*Cottleston, Cottleston,
Cottleston Pie,
A fly can't bird, but
a bird can fly.
Ask me a riddle
and I reply:
"Cottleston,
Cottleston,
Cottleston Pie."*

*Cottleston, Cottleston, Cottleston Pie,
A fish can't whistle and neither can I.
Ask me a riddle and I reply:*
"Cottleston, Cottleston,
Cottleston Pie."

*Cottleston, Cottleston, Cottleston Pie,
Why does a chicken, I don't know why.
Ask me a riddle and I reply:*
"Cottleston, Cottleston,
Cottleston Pie."

So Owl wrote . . . and this is what he wrote:

HIPY PAPY BTHUTHDTH THUTHDA BTHUTHDY.

Pooh looked on admiringly. "I'm just saying 'A Happy Birthday'," said Owl carelessly. "It's a nice long one," said Pooh, very much impressed by it.

Piglet was sitting on the ground at the door of his house blowing happily at a dandelion, and wondering whether it would be this year, next year, sometime or never. He had just discovered that it would be never, and was trying to remember what "*it*" was, and hoping it wasn't anything nice . . .

Of course Pooh would be with him, and it was much more Friendly with two.

"Hallo, Rabbit," he said,
"is that you?"
"Let's pretend it isn't,"
said Rabbit, "and see
what happens."

"Oh, Eeyore, you *are* wet!" said Piglet, feeling him. Eeyore shook himself, and asked somebody to explain to Piglet what happened when you had been inside a river for quite a long time.

"Well," said Pooh, "it's the middle of the night, which is a good time for going to sleep. And tomorrow

morning we'll have some honey for breakfast. Do Tiggers like honey?" "They like everything," said Tigger cheerfully.

"Tiggers don't like honey."

"Oh!" said Pooh, and tried to make it sound Sad and Regretful. "I thought they liked everything."

"Hallo, Piglet. This is Tigger."
"Oh, is it?" said Piglet, and he edged round to the other side of the table.
"I thought Tiggers were smaller than that."
"Not the big ones," said Tigger.
"They like haycorns," said Pooh, "so that's what we've come for, because poor Tigger hasn't had any breakfast yet."

After a long munching noise . . . he said firmly: "Tiggers don't like haycorns."
"But you said they liked everything except honey," said Pooh.
"Everything except honey and haycorns," explained Tigger.

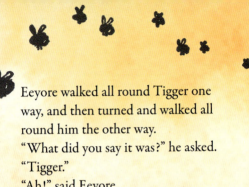

Eeyore walked all round Tigger one way, and then turned and walked all round him the other way.
"What did you say it was?" he asked.
"Tigger."
"Ah!" said Eeyore.

"He's just come," explained Piglet.
"Ah!" said Eeyore again.
He thought for a long time and then said:
"When is he going?"

Pooh explained to Eeyore that Tigger was a great friend of Christopher Robin's, who had come to stay in the Forest, and Piglet explained to Tigger that he mustn't mind what Eeyore said because he was *always* gloomy;

and Eeyore explained to Piglet that, on the contrary, he was feeling particularly cheerful this morning; and Tigger explained to anybody who was listening that he hadn't had any breakfast yet.

"What's the matter?" asked Pooh.
"*Hot!*" mumbled Tigger.

~~~~~~~~~

"But you said," began Pooh—
"you *said* that Tiggers liked
everything except honey and
haycorns."
"*And* thistles," said Tigger . . .

"Now, Roo, dear, remember what you promised."
"What is it?" whispered Tigger to Piglet.
"His Strengthening Medicine," said Piglet. "He hates it."

So Tigger came closer, and he leant over the back of Roo's chair, and suddenly he put out his tongue, and took one large golollop ... and a peaceful smile came over his face as he said, "So *that's* what Tiggers like!"

"Hallo, Eeyore," said Christopher Robin, as he opened the door and came out. "How are *you*?"

"It's snowing still," said Eeyore gloomily.

"So it is."

"*And* freezing."

"Is it?"

"Yes," said Eeyore. "However," he said, brightening up a little, "we haven't had an earthquake lately."

"After all," said Rabbit to himself, "Christopher Robin depends on Me. He's fond of Pooh and Piglet and Eeyore, and so am I, but they haven't any Brain. Not to notice. And he respects Owl, because you can't help respecting anybody who can spell TUESDAY, even if he doesn't spell it right; but spelling isn't everything."

By the time it came to the edge of the Forest the stream had grown up, so that it was almost a river, and, being grown-up, it did not run and jump and sparkle along as it used to do when it was younger, but moved more slowly. For it knew now where it was going, and it said to itself, "There is no hurry. We shall get there some day."

Christopher Robin came down from the Forest to the bridge, feeling all sunny and careless, and just as if twice nineteen didn't matter a bit, as it didn't on such a happy afternoon, and he thought that if he stood on the bottom rail of the bridge, and leant over, and watched the river slipping slowly away beneath him, then he would suddenly know everything that there was to be known, and he would be able to tell Pooh, who wasn't quite sure about some of it.

The wind was against them now, and Piglet's ears streamed behind him like banners as he fought his way along, and it seemed hours before he got them into the shelter of the Hundred Acre Wood and they stood up straight again, to listen, a little nervously, to the roaring of the gale among the treetops.

"Supposing a tree fell down, Pooh, when we were underneath it?"

"Supposing it didn't," said Pooh after careful thought.

Pooh looked proud at being called a stout and helpful bear, and said modestly that he just happened to think of it.

"Sing Ho! for the life of a Bear!"

"I shall sing that first line twice, and perhaps if I sing it very quickly, I shall find myself singing the third and fourth lines before I have time to think of them, and that will be a Good Song."

Sing Ho! for the life of a Bear!
Sing Ho! for the life of a Bear!
I don't much mind if it rains or snows,
'Cos I've got a lot of honey on my nice new nose,
I don't much care if it snows or thaws,
'Cos I've got a lot of honey on my nice clean paws!
Sing Ho! for a Bear!
Sing Ho! for a Pooh!
And I'll have a little something in an hour or two.

"If this is flying I shall

"What I like best in the whole world is Me and Piglet going to see You, and You saying 'What about a little something?' and Me saying, 'Well, I shouldn't mind a little something, should you, Piglet,' and it being a hummy sort of day outside, and birds singing."

Pooh began to feel a little more comfortable, because when you are a Bear of Very Little Brain, and you Think of Things, you find sometimes that a Thing which seemed very Thingish inside you is quite different when it gets out into the open and has other people looking at it.

"How do you do Nothing?" asked Pooh, after he had wondered for a long time.

"Well, it's when people call out at you just as you're going off to do it, What are you going to do, Christopher Robin, and you say, Oh, nothing, and then you go and do it."

"When you wake up in the morning, Pooh," said Piglet at last, "what's the first thing you say to yourself?"

"What's for breakfast?" said Pooh. "What do *you* say, Piglet?"

"I say, I wonder what's going to happen exciting *today*?" said Piglet.

Pooh nodded thoughtfully. "It's the same thing," he said.

But, of course, it isn't really Good-bye, because the Forest will always be there . . . and anybody who is Friendly with Bears can find it.